PEACE
Within Her Painting

Patrick Madden

I would like to dedicate this story to the lovely Julia Holland and her sleepless nights. I would also like to thank her for providing her wonderful artwork for the cover.

"Peace Within Her Painting" by Patrick Madden. ISBN 978-1-947532-68-7 (hardcover).

Published 2018 by Virtualbookworm.com Publishing Inc., P.O. Box 9949, College Station, TX 77842, US. ©2018, Patrick Madden.

All rights reserved. No part of this publication may be reproduced, stored in a retrieval system, or transmitted in any form or by any means, electronic, mechanical, recording or otherwise, without the prior written permission of Patrick Madden.

Peace Within Her Painting

IT WAS ALMOST MIDNIGHT and the end of a beautiful summer's day in Blaenavon. It was a warm night and Julia Holland, a married, middle-aged, self-taught artist from Forgeside Estate, was sitting on the banks of Forge pond, not far from where she lived. Julia, for the past few years, had been having trouble sleeping and would be up awake every night. She had tried all kinds of herbal treatments her local doctor and friends suggested, but unfortunately, they were of no real use to her. If she dropped off to sleep at all, she would be awake again in less than fifteen minutes, crying. As a result, she became very depressed and weary looking. To help her through these sleepless nights Julia would turn over another page in her sketchbook and would paint what she thought were the loveliest things she had seen that day. Her paintings were plain and simple but very captivating.

Now on this particular warm summer's night, there was such a beautiful bright full moon that Julia had decided to take a walk up to the pond where she played as a child. While sitting there, she began thinking about those days.

"I was happy then," she said quietly. "I had no worries and slept all night."

With those memories lingering in her mind she began to cry and raised her tearful face up towards the heavens and the brightly shining moon.

"Why! Why can't I sleep?" she asked sadly. "It's making me so unhappy and miserable."

Julia stayed there crying with her tearful face now buried in a pretty handkerchief until she felt a cold breeze that made her stand up. It was a chilly breeze and with the town clock striking the hour of midnight she decided it was time to go home. Then, as she turned to go, she noticed that on the pond there was a perfect reflection of the moon as if the water was a mirror. She hadn't seen anything like this and couldn't understand how it could be because the whole pond was now violently rippling from the breeze. In disbelief she rubbed her eyes, thinking they were playing tricks, but as she looked again the refection was still there even brighter than before. It was so bright that she put her hand out to shade her eyes. Then, as she did so, she suddenly felt a tingle in her left hand and a warm feeling up her arm. The moment she felt this, the moon disappeared behind a cloud leaving the Forge pond in darkness. By the time she wiggled her fingers and rubbed her arm, the bright moon was back from behind the cloud again, only this time there was no clear reflection on the water.

"Ah, I knew it was my eyes, all the time," she said to herself and headed off back down past Big Pit, the towns' Colliery and home to her bed.

In the morning, which was Saturday, Julia said nothing to her husband, Mark, about her experience. Well, after all, he wouldn't have been too happy about her being up there in the early hours, all alone. Nevertheless, she did later mention it to her mother, who was definitely not very pleased about her being out at that time of night.

"Yes, you must have the same eyes as your father," her mother said. "He sometimes sees things that are not really there. I've told him to have his eyes tested but he's so stubborn."

With that, Julia laughed, headed home, picked up her sketchbook, paints and crayons and went up to the flower park to sit and paint. It was another hot day so she decided to sit underneath the shade of the willow tree where it was cooler. Blaenavon Rugby ground was adjacent to the park and normally there would be a rugby match going on but as it was summer there weren't any, though there were a few lads kicking the ball around. Then, as Julia was sat there wondering what to paint, she heard a rattle above her and a rugby ball and a pile of leaves dropped down beside her. She picked up the ball just as Arthur Parry was climbing over the gate to fetch it.

"Ah, Julia," he said as she came out from under the tree. "Can we have our ball back please?" He jokingly asked.

"Well, just this once," she replied trying not to laugh. "But if it happens again, I'm keeping it."

They both laughed. Arthur then went off to join his pals leaving Julia to go back under the tree to think. After picking up her book she noticed that leaves had fallen onto the page she had opened and they were in the formation of a flower.

"Well, that's a coincidence," she said to herself. "That's what I'll do. I'll paint the flower gardens."

With that decision made, Julia went and sat on one of the park benches. There were five flower gardens in all, so she thought that one a day would be a nice project and to paint them on the same page would be lovely. Her sketchbook pages, if she was careful, were large enough. So, after roughly setting out five sections on her page, Julia began to paint.

There were children in the park, some walking along with their parent's others were playing around behind her. Julia took no notice of them and they didn't bother her either. In fact, no one even spoke to her, which she was very happy about for she was concentrating and really didn't want to be disturbed.

In a couple of hours, a happy Julia had finished her first flower bed and was very pleased with the result.

"I'd better go home now. Mark will be worrying about me," she said while packing things away in her bag.

Then, as she turned to walk away she heard a man from the other side of the flower beds call out.

"It's a beautiful day today and the flowers look so lovely, don't you think?" He asked.

Julia looked and could see that the man was a priest belonging to some kind of religious organisation. He had white hair down to his shoulders and his dark clothes were very strange looking.

"Yes, it is a beautiful day and the flowers are very pretty," remarked Shirley Allen who was walking behind her.

"Oh, I thought he was talking to me," she muttered and walked quickly on.

When Julia arrived home she was relieved to find Mark fast asleep in the garden. That gave her the opportunity to prepare the tea before waking him.

That night, before they went to bed, Julia showed mark her latest painting and told him about her project. Mark thought the painting was nice and as long as she was happy doing it he didn't mind and would have the dinner ready for her tomorrow when she came home.

"That'll be a first," she said to herself. "I'll believe it when I see it."

Julia, as usual, didn't get a good night's rest and was happy to get out of bed and have her breakfast. Once again the weather was fine and according to the forecast, it was staying that way for many days to come. So, early that afternoon Julia set off to the park for the second stage of her exciting project. She was tired by the time she reached the park bench, but a little happier than she had been. So with her pencil, brush and paints, she began painting the second flower bed.

While taking a rest from her work, she noticed the same religious person walking around the flower beds admiring the flowers. As he passed by, he put his hand up to her and she acknowledged him with a smile. He had a very kind and peaceful face that made her think.

"Oh, he must be so happy. It must be nice to be like that."

She watched him go around the corner and out of sight before picking up her brush to finish off the final touches.

With that done she was away home to a nice surprise.

"Good gracious. I don't believe it," she said to herself. "He's been and made the dinner."

Mark had stayed true to his word. He had made the dinner, even though it was only fish fingers, egg and peas. It wasn't exactly a Sunday roast or even a good combination but it was edible and she was hungry. But, thankfully, Mark was only joking, he had her dinner put away in the oven.

The following day, before Julia went away to the park, she made up a pot of stew that would simmer away and be ready when she came home.

So, away she went to another afternoon at the park that concluded in another delightful and very successful day of painting. Yes, and she was very pleased with how her project was shaping up. It was almost four o'clock and plenty of time before Mark came home at six. So she hurried off and made sure she didn't stop to talk on the way.

After tea, Julia showed her husband how she was progressing with her painting. Mark was pleased with it and told her so.

"It's coming along nicely, my girl," he said giving her a light tap on the hand. "Yes, I really mean it. You are doing a fine job. It will certainly look nice when it's finished."

Hearing Mark say this, cheered her up immensely, though it didn't help her much with her insomnia. She was in and out of bed sweating streams, pacing around the house trying to think of something or someway to help her sleep. The only thing that did assist and comfort her was after drawing and painting a picture. But, even then, it was only a matter of a couple of hours before she would wake again, to her dismay.

It was Tuesday and day four of her project, but Julia was in two minds about going to the park that day. She was so tired that if it wasn't for the fact she loved her days there she would have quite happily stayed at home.

"Ah, I'll have a nice cup of tea with plenty of sugar before I go," she thought. "I'll be alright when I get there. I'll take some biscuits with me for a snack."

So after that sweet cup of tea, she headed off to what now seemed to be her favourite place; the park. As she made her way up through Charles Street, Julia spotted the strange Priest again. He was sitting on a bench at the top of Charles Street Green, reading a little book. She put her head down and walked on, thinking.

"Where is he from, I wonder?" she asked herself. "What kind of church and parish does he belonged to? I have never seen anyone dressed like him before."

Putting that to the back of her mind, Julia sat down and started the fourth section of her five-day painting. Now, because of the different kind and arrangement of flowers, she found this next flowerbed a tough one to captivate. Some were tall and droopy while others were small and hard to see. It was a difficult feat, to say the least, but she relished the challenge and was pleased with the final result and went away home, happy enough.

While Julia was away at the park, her mother had called in to see how she was feeling and left a note asking her to call up after tea.

"Hi Mam," said Julia as she opened her mother's door that evening. "Is there anything wrong?"

"No," replied her mother. "I was just wondering how you were. But my goodness, Julia, you look so drawn and tired. Do you ever sleep at all?"

"Ah, don't worry, Mam. I'll be okay before long. Just you wait and see," she replied in hope that she would.

"Oh, I don't know, Julia," her mother said while shaking her head. "You've been saying this for a couple years now."

"Ah don't worry Mam. Come on, I'll make us up a nice cup of tea. Do you want one Dad?"

So Julia made up a pot of tea while her mother fetched the cups and biscuits. Then later, as all three were sitting down chatting, Julia mentioned to her father about the strangely dressed Priest she had seen a couple of times. She wondered if he knew there was a new Priest or Vicar in town.

"No, not that I know of," he replied. "If there were, I would have surely known by now. No, he must be from out of town. Although going by the way you described his clothes, it's quite possible he's from another country."

That was that solved and Julia thought no more about it.

It was time to go now, so Julia kissed and wished her parents goodnight and went home. Mark was out playing crib up at the club, so she went off to bed.

Surprisingly, Julia went to sleep immediately though only for a couple of hours. Mark, even being as quiet as he could, still managed to wake her from her slumber. After that it was the same old routine, tossing and turning until she went downstairs to enable Mark to get some rest. He had to be up at five to start work at six so she had his breakfast ready and his sandwiches made when he came down. With breakfast finished, Mark set off down the road with one of his workmates while Julia watched and waved from the door.

The house was tidy enough and that was a good thing. Julia, as we know, could not sleep for any length of time, but she had great satisfaction in sitting down, doing nothing.

The afternoon couldn't come quickly enough for her and when it did, she took the bus downtown as far as Market Street and walked from there up to the park.

It was the last day of her little project and she was looking forward to finishing it, though after sitting down looking at it, it seemed another difficult task, even more so than the day before. Nevertheless, Julia was not deterred. In fact, it was another challenge for her. She thought the only way to gain experience and to progress in her love of painting was overcome all these obstacles. So, with that in mind, she began to finish what was soon to become her very own masterpiece.

It took her longer than she would have liked because of the fact many children were in the park that day and their screams and shouts constantly disturbed her concentration. It was only when some of the children went off to play on the swings did she get some peace to carry on and finally finish it. She then sighed and sat back, held out her painting and smiled.

"Whoa, that last one was really tough," she said looking at her painting. "But there again, I suppose nothing is easy."

"Yes, young lady, you are quite right. Nothing in life is easy," said a person sitting at the other end of her bench.

It was the Priest. Julia knew there was someone sitting there but was so deep in concentration that she didn't bother to see who it was and then forgot the person was even there.

"Ooh, hello, Sir," said Julia. "I'm sorry but I was talking to myself. I've just finished a painting of these flower beds and I am extremely happy with it.

"Yes, you should be, because I think it's beautiful. You must be a very religious lady?" He then asked.

"Oh no, not me, Sir," she replied. "Well I am, though not very. But what makes you think I am?"

"It's your painting. I see it in your painting," he replied with a smile.

"What! In my painting?" She asked looking at it again. "I see nothing. Only flowers."

"Yes, but if you look at the red ones you will see what I see," said the kind-faced Priest.

So, Julia looked in each bed of flowers and studied all the red ones.

"Ooh that's incredible, Sir," she said in disbelief. "All my red flowers form a letter and every bed that I painted has one. I don't believe it. Oh, Sir, they spell out the name of 'Jesus' in a way as if it had been signed."

"Yes, that's what I saw and doesn't it look really lovely?" asked the Priest.

"Yes, but I don't understand, Sir because I didn't mean to do it."

"Well, perhaps it was meant to be," said the Priest. "Now, as I am looking at your painting, it reminds me of something I suggested to a young boy on one of my travels. He was troubled at night with bad dreams, that all children have, but this particular boy would lose a lot of sleep because of it. So I told him to write out in red the name of 'Jesus' and keep it under his pillow. Then at night, whatever his troubles, whether it be from dreams or just he couldn't sleep, he should whisper out the name of Jesus and he would come to comfort him."

"Who are you, Sir?" Julia asked curiously. "I had never seen you before until I started my painting?"

"My name is John Vianney from Ars," he replied. "And my advice to you young lady is, take heed of what is in your painting and place the name of 'Jesus' under your pillow. It helped the young boy and if you have faith in what I tell you, it will help you too."

Julia was fascinated by this kind soft spoken Priest and was quite happy listening to him.

"There is one more thing I would like to say before I leave you to pack," said the priest. "Every morning, the very moment you open your eyes, offer up to 'Jesus' all the lovely things you will hear, see and do that day. Now with that in mind, wouldn't it be nice to offer him all your lovely paintings. There's no need to keep them because Jesus will have them waiting for you in Heaven. Now, on that note, I must bid you goodbye. I have enjoyed talking to you so much, Julia."

"Oh no, Sir. Don't go. Wait a minute. Let me pack and if you are going downtown I'll walk with you," said Julia as she began to pack.

But when she had finished and turned to face him, he was gone.

"Oh, no! Where is he?" She cried. "Hello. Where are you? Where are you Sir and how do you know my name?"

There was no reply so she ran out the park gates looking for him, but alas, he was nowhere to be seen. Julia was disappointed but at the same time had a feeling she hadn't felt for a long time. She was happy. For how long she didn't care. Right now, she couldn't wait to tell Mark and her mother all about her painting and the Priest she met that afternoon.

So, Julia hurried home to make the tea which she had hot and ready on the table when Mark came home from work. By then, although still excited, she didn't know how to tell her husband about her painting and her eventful afternoon. She felt he wouldn't believe that she had unintentionally painted the word Jesus in her painting. After all, she couldn't even believe it herself. So she was a little nervous about telling him, especially about the strange Priest and what he said.

"Well, Julia," said Mark after she had washed up and he had read the paper. "Did you finish your painting?"

"Yes, I did. Would you like to see it?" She asked, nervously.

"Of course I would," he replied. "Show me, but let me find my glasses first."

"They are on top of your head," she said as she went to fetch her painting.

"Oh, yes, so they are. Well, that saves me going looking for them," he said and laughed.

"Now Julia, let me see this painting of yours," he said as she handed it to him.

"Well, well, Julia. I would say that this is your best one yet," he remarked. "It's lovely and the colours are beautiful. You've even put little butterflies and bees in there too. Yes, it's very nice my dear. It really is."

Julia was happy that he liked it but she had to ask him if he noticed something about the red flowers.

"Oh yes, I see," he said as he studied them. "They are letters and you have written the word Jesus in your painting. What made you do that?"

"I don't know. I didn't mean to do it. It just happened to be there when I finished."

She was about to tell Mark about the Priest but stopped herself. The Priest was too difficult to explain plus Mark wouldn't have been very happy with her talking to a strange person who came and sat by her on a park bench.

"Well, I don't know what to say, Julia," said Mark shaking his head. "It's going to take some believing I can tell you because there is no way those letters could have been created in such detail if it wasn't intentional. Otherwise, all I can say is, you must have a Divine touch," he added and laughed.

Julia knew it would take some believing and was happy she didn't mention the Priest. So she put her painting away and sat down with Mark to listen to Blaenavon Male Voice Choir on the radio. As you know most of their songs are hymns, so that made Julia think of the Priest again and what he talked about.

"Where did he say he was from?" she asked herself. "Ars, that's what he said. He must be a Priest from Ars."

So, that night, while lying in bed, Julia asked Mark if he knew of a country or a place called Ars. He had never heard of it. So she thought perhaps that in the morning it would be a good idea to pop down to Saint Peters Church, maybe the Reverend Rufus would know something about him.

Julia slept very little and was already up to send her husband off to work. With that done, she made herself some toast and coffee then sat down to listen to the radio. She couldn't wait to show her mother the painting, but once again, wasn't going to mention the Priest. So at ten o'clock when her parents would have finished their breakfast, she popped over to show and explain all about her extraordinary painting.

Her parents, although they believed their daughter, said very much the same as Mark. It was totally unbelievable for anyone else to think it true. Nevertheless, they loved her painting and just as her husband Mark had thought, it was by far her best one yet.

"Oh thank you, Mam and Dad," she said and kissed them. "I'm so pleased you like it and that you believe me. Oh, I'm so happy I could scream."

"Uh, uh, not in this house you won't," said her father. "I'm deaf enough now with all your mother's nagging."

"Oh, you! A little more nagging I should be doing if you ask me," said her mother, giving him a clout.

That was funny and it made Julia laugh. She laughed so much that her parents laughed too.

"Well, I had better be going now, Mam," said Julia picking up her bag. "I am off for a walk downtown."

So, Julia said goodbye and walked off through the estate, downtown to the Church House. There was no answer, so she went around to the Church and found Pamela Watts cleaning and polishing the candlesticks.

"Ooh, hello Julia. I haven't seen you for a long time. If you've come to help, I'm finished," she said and smiled.

"No," replied Julia. "I wanted to ask the Reverend something but he isn't in."

"Yes, he's out of town today. Can I help?" asked Pamela.

"Maybe you can," Julia replied. "I was in town yesterday and met a Priest. He said his name was John Vianney or something like that. Do you know him? Is he new around here?"

Pamela stopped to ponder. She had heard the name but wanted a moment to think.

"Well, Julia. The only priest I know by the name of John Vianney would be the French Priest they called the Curè d' Ars. He was a very holy man indeed, but he died in the eighteen hundreds, almost two hundred years ago. Are you sure that was the name he gave you?"

"Oh, I could have mistaken him," said Julia. "Perhaps I'll see him again and make sure next time. Thank you, Pamela, and by the way, the church is looking really lovely and I see you are making good progress in the cleaning up of the Cemetery. It was so sad to see how the church had disrespected our ancestors by neglecting it for so long. So well done Pamela. Goodbye, for now, I'm off to the Library."

She left Pamela to finish her work and went around to the Library which was situated in the Heritage Centre. If John Vianney was dead and being such a holy man, then there should be something written about him. So, Julia searched through the French religious section that recounted the lives of Holy people in 19th century. There were a few to choose from but it was in the fifth book that Julia found what she was looking for and gasped.

"That's him! That's definitely him," she said looking at the Priest's picture. "He's a Saint. A real Saint. Oh, Mam, he's a Saint and I was talking to him. I don't believe it."

Julia was so overwhelmed she felt faint, passed out and came around sitting on a chair.

"Are you alright Julia," asked Kay Thomas offering her some water. "You frightened the living daylights out of me. One minute you were talking to yourself and the next you were flat out on the floor. Annette said you are the second person to have fainted here this week."

"Yes, I'm okay," replied Julia. "I'm sorry I frightened you. I have never fainted before in my life. It must be the weather. Oh, what time is it? I'll have to be going, I've nothing for tea."

"You just sit there until the colour comes back in those cheeks of yours," said Kay patting Julia's hands. "Annette and I volunteered to look after the Library this week, so while you are recovering, I'll stamp the book you were looking at. If that's the one you want, that is?"

"No, I was just looking at it, that's all. I don't want to take it home. But honestly, Kay, I'm okay and I had better go."

"Give it five more minutes," said Annette as she handed Julia her bag. "We don't want you fainting off again, now do we?"

Julia was okay but she could see that Kay and Annette were worried so she stayed for five minutes before thanking them and heading home.

On her way, she couldn't help chuckling to herself. She wasn't afraid that she had seen the Curè d' Ars. In fact, she felt honoured that he had appeared to her and was hoping perhaps, he would again. No one would ever believe her, but she didn't care because no one was ever going to know. It was her little secret and she was keeping it. Her painting was now her pride and joy and was going to do as the Priest suggested.

That evening, Julia went upstairs with a red crayon and a blank calling card which she thought very appropriate and carefully painted the name 'JESUS' across it. Then, after slipping it under her pillow she went downstairs. Mark was very pleased how happy she looked and complimented her.

"Well love, I must say, ever since you began that painting of yours you've been looking a lot happier and I really mean it. In a matter of a couple of days, you are beginning to be your old self again. Are you going to do any more of those paintings?"

"Yes I am," she replied. "And I know what I am going to do with them too."

"Well good for you love and I'm pleased for you. Who knows, you could be famous one day and perhaps someone will write your story. That will be something, eh?"

"Thank you, Mark. It would be nice, but I very much doubt it," she said and kissed him.

"Oh aye, I'm getting a kiss now am I?" He said jokingly. "I normally only get one a week."

"Ooh, you little fibber you. It's the other way around. I'm lucky if I get a peck on the eye," she replied and they burst out laughing.

At the end of the night and after a cup of cocoa, they made their way to bed. Mark was soon off to asleep, so as Julia was lying there she put her hand under her pillow, touch her little calling card and sighed.

"I'm not expecting any miracles and I don't deserve any," she whispered. "But can you just please help me sleep, even if it's only an hour or two more than usual. I also thought I'd tell you that I have decided to offer up my paintings to you. What for I don't know, but your Priest thought it a good idea. Now, please don't think I am trying to bribe you, but that's what he suggested I do."

She then quietly slipped out of bed, picked up her painting and went outside to another beautiful, starry, half-moonlit night. Julia smiled and as she gazed up into the heavens, raised her painting high towards the moon just as the town clock was striking the midnight hour. At that very moment, the lovely Julia sighed as she remembered the night up at the Forge Pond. So, with tiny little tears of joy rolling down her now rosy cheeks, she smiled and whispered, "Thank you, Sir."

6th January 2018

www.ingramcontent.com/pod-product-compliance
Lightning Source LLC
Chambersburg PA
CBHW071917160426
42813CB00098B/461